VINTAGE

HOLIDAY

BAKING RECIPES

Edited by Maggie Mack

Library of Congress Cataloging-in-Publication Data
MacKinnon, KM Vintage Holiday Baking Recipes/Maggie Mack/KM MacKinnon.
1st ed. p. cm.
ISBN ISBN-13: 978-0615572932
ISBN-10: 0615572936
1. Cooking / Holiday

Printed in the United States of America
First Edition

audentes fortuna juva

Grandma always said "you can do magic with a pound of butter, a pound of flour and a pound of sugar!"

The book you are holding in your hands contains recipes from my grandmother's shelf including some old fashioned baking notes. Simple, Warm, and Delicious!

Back when our grandparents and great-grandparents were young they learned how to bake using the most basic ingredients, in the simplest manner. I don't remember my grandmother adding a million different ingredients into her baked goods. What I do remember were yummy, warm cakes and cookies that not only filled my stomach, but also filled my soul.

Forget about all the artificial baking goods, artificial ingredients and artificial trappings of today's baked goods available to us in the store.

Instead, this year, and every year, let's embrace and re-discover the old way of baking. The simple and delicious way with "a pound of sugar, a pound of flour and a pound of butter."

Happy Holidays and Happy Baking!!!

THOUGHTS ON BREAD MAKING & BAKING

In the making of bread-stuffs, there are so many conditions to contend with that it is absolutely impossible to give any set rule.

In fact there may be two mills in a town each making flour from practically the same wheat. You may be able to make good goods from the flour of one
mill, and impossible to even make fair goods with flour from the other.

Again it is impossible to suit the tastes of every person.

Therefore the recipes in this book have been ar- ranged so they may be changed to a certain extent to suit the taste and materials of the individuals.

By far the most important part of bread making is to get a knowledge of it. Give it part of your time
and some study and by using good judgment you will then succeed. Failure is lack of knowledge, success is the result of knowledge.

Cleanliness is a very important part of the success of baking, keep every thing clean, you will then have no trouble in turning out a good sweet loaf.

If the flour you are using is giving good
satisfaction stick to it. The same may be
said of yeast and other ingredients. But
if they are not good do not hesitate to
make a change.

Do not rush your doughs and work them up
when they are not ready, it will only mean
failure or partial failure.

Good hot oven does not mean red hot. It
means an oven that has been properly
heated to a certain degree so it will do
good baking.

Do not put your bread in the oven to bake
and then commence heating your stove, and
wonder why your bread is soggy and heavy.
Have the oven the right temperature and
keep it that way.

Take less yeast and more salt in summer or
warm weather and more yeast and a little
less salt in winter or cold weather.

Always keep flour in a warm — not hot —
dry place.

Always keep yeast in a dry cool place.

If bread, rolls or biscuit are washed
immediately after baking with melted
butter or lard it will shine nicely and
make the crust much softer.

If you wish to put a gloss on your bread,
rolls or biscuit take a little corn starch
and dissolve in cold water, add boiling
water until thick enough to spread under
brush.

If you can not mould dough into loaves you
will find the following way very easy to
learn. Cut or weigh your dough into the
size you want your loaf to be. Turn the
smoothest side down on the bread board,
press out flat with the hands, lap in the
sides and mash, commence at end farthest
from you and roll it up, just as though
you were rolling up jelly roll, when you
get to the end mash together, roll
under the hands until you get it the
desired length, then put in pan joined
placed down, leaving smooth side up.

To shape rolls grease the hands with a
little lard or butter, then pinch off a
piece of dough the size of a small egg,
roll between the hands until round.

It will improve the crust on bread, if
before you put it in the oven you will
grease the top of it with melted lard or
butter.

Always sift flour before using it.

To tell good flour from bad, take a small
amount of flour and lay on the hand, take
a knife and make smooth, if it has a cream

like color it is good but if you see red
and black specks in it, it isn't good.

Milk can be used in bread, rolls, coffee
cakes, instead of water, and it improves
the goods very much, when milk is used in
making sponge it should always
be boiled and cooled to temperature
desired.

The strength of baking powder varies so
much with the different brands that it is
impossible to state just how much to use.
The only way to be successful is, to get a
certain brand and learn to use it, that is
learn how much to take then stick to that
brand.

MATERIALS USED IN BREAD MAKING

To make bread making easier it will first
be very necessary to give the reader some
information on the materials used and to
acquaint her with the troubles of bread
making so they can be avoided, thereby
making success sure.

Flour

By far the most important ingredient in
bread making is flour.

There are two kinds (but many brands) of
white flour. Spring or hard wheat flour
and winter or soft wheat flour.

Spring or hard wheat flour is flour made
from wheat sown in the spring. The flour
is hard coarse grained and strong, it is
therefore best adapted for bread making.
While it can be used for pastry and
cakes it is not near so good as winter or
soft wheat flour.

Winter or soft wheat flour is made from
wheat sown in the fall, and is soft and of
very fine grain, it is not strong, it is
therefore best adapted to. pastry and cake
making. It can be used in making bread but
is not as good as spring wheat flour.
It is therefore necessary if you wish the
best results in the making of bread that
you use a good grade of spring or hard
wheat flour.

Water

Next to flour the most important
ingredient is water, the water used should
be fresh and clean. Soft water soaks up
flour more thoroughly and quicker
than hard water and is therefore better.

Salt

The salt used should be clean and of a
good quality, coarse salt can be used and
gives satisfaction, but fine salt
dissolves quicker and better and
consequently is better.

Sugar

Any good grade of sugar whether it be
granulated or brown will give satisfactory
results.

Lard

The lard used should be of a good quality
and should be warmed until it is soft.

Yeast

If you are using a yeast that is giving
you satisfactory results then by all means
stick to it. There will be found elsewhere
in this book several recipes for making
yeast. All of which are good and if made
as directed will give excellent results.

SOME THINGS TO AVOID

Although you may have selected a good
flour and the rest of your materials may
be first class in every respect, it is
still possible to make a failure of your
bread. Now in order to avoid making a
failure after a selection of good
materials, it will be necessary to guard
against such troubles as sour bread, spots
in bread and ropey places in bread, each
will be dealt with separately and the
cause of each and how to avoid the cause.

Sour Bread

Sour bread is by far the most frequent cause of poor bread stuffs.

There are several causes of sourness.

1st. The cook or housewife will make her dough in a bowl or vessel that has some old dough or other
foreign matter in it which has become sour, the dough soon takes up this sourness and once in the dough it
works rapidly and the result is your bread stuffs is not good, it is more or less sour.

To avoid this sourness thoroughly clean the bowl or vessel and give it a good airing.

2nd. In making your dough you will get it too warm thus causing the yeast cells to work so rapidly that they work themselves to death, then sourness takes place and your bread stuff is sure to be a sour failure. To avoid this all that is necessary is to be extra careful and not get your dough too warm, dough should be made lukewarm in summer and blood warm in winter. A little practice and being careful is all that is necessary to get the temperature right, it is easy to learn and you will soon get it.

3rd. In making the dough you get it too

cold, and then set it close to the fire
leaving one side of it to the fire too
long, it getting too warm, the yeast cells
in the warm dough work themselves to death
causing sourness to start up, then when
you work up your dough to make it into
loaves you work the sour dough all through
the other dough, consequently your bread
is sour in places. To avoid this do not
let one side of your dough stay towards
the fire but turn your bowl or vessel
around a little every once and awhile.

Spots in bread are caused either from the
dough getting too warm in one place as
just described, causing sour bread in
spots, but in case of spots the dough gets
so sour that it turns dark, or in mixing
you do not thoroughly mix, leaving hard
lumps in the dough, the yeast cells do not
have much affect on these lumps
consequently they do not whiten or get
soft and the result is lumps in your
bread. To avoid spots treat same as to
avoid sourness and mix dough thoroughly.

The cause of rope in bread is still
puzzling many good bakers, but after
careful study it is found to be
more or less caused from the flour,
therefore if you are bothered with rope in
your bread the best thing to do is to try
a new brand of flour.

HOME MADE YEAST

Where bread is baked regularly say once or
twice a week or oftener you will find this
yeast to be a good one.

One medium size or two small potatoes.
Three tablespoons flour.
Three tablespoonful sugar.
One tablespoon salt.
Yeast.

Add enough water to make two quarts.
Peel and wash potato, boil in sufficient
water until soft, take potato out and put
in another bowl or vessel, letting water
cool, thoroughly wash the potato, add
flour and mix, add sugar and mix, add salt
and mix, to this add the water the potato
was boiled in and mix, dissolve one yeast
cake in about half pint water (any brand
of yeast will do,) (this is only to
get the new yeast dissolved to ferment)
add the dissolved yeast, then add enough
water to make two quarts more or less of
yeast, the temperature should be blood
warm in cold weather and lukewarm in warm
weather, let yeast stand nine to twelve
hours when it will be ready for use.

The above is for the start or first time
you make the yeast. For making the yeast
the second time and thereafter observe the
following : Just before you use the yeast
take out one pint, (for convenience put it
in pint self sealer and keep in cool, dry
place) then when you make your yeast the

second time put in the pint you took out
and saved instead of the yeast cake.

Always save out one pint to put in the
next making.

You will find it very convenient if you
will make this yeast at night and let set
until next morning when it will be ready
to use.

Dry Hop Yeast

Take half pound hops and boil in little
more than two quarts water until hops
begin to sink, put a quart of good flour,
one-half cup sugar, one-fourth cup salt
in a basin, strain the liquor from the
hops into the flour, sugar and salt,
boiling hot and stir it. If too thin add
enough flour to make a stiff batter ; be
sure the flour is well scalded, or it will
not keep as long. When lukewarm mix into
it three to six cakes of dry yeast
dissolved in a little water, number of
cakes depending on the size or two ounces
compressed yeast dissolved in a little
water. Cover it and let stand about twelve
hours or until it has risen and fallen,
then mix in enough cornmeal to make a
dough and let it rise again, then roll out
about half an inch thick and cut into two
and a half inch squares, and dry in the
sun. It will take three to five days to
dry, and must be turned every day and
taken in in the evening. It will then be

ready for use.

TO MAKE BREAD FROM HOME MADE YEAST

Take the home made yeast when ready and
mix in enough flour to make a moderately
stiff sponge, let rise until blubbers form
and break, the sponge will then be ready
to make into dough, if the sponge is not
the right temperature add enough water to
make it so, add about half pound soft or
melted lard and mix well, then mix in
enough flour to make a good dough. If
winter wheat flour is used make a stiff
dough and if spring wheat flour is used,
make a soft dough. When dough is the
proper stiffness, turn out of bowl or
vessel on board and knead for ten to
twenty minutes, working in all scraps,
leaving the dough firm and smooth, put the
dough back in the bowl or vessel and
let rise. If you will notice when dough is
first made it is firm and if you press
your fist in it and take it out the dough
will come back more or less. But when
the dough has risen to such extent that
when you push your fist down in it, and
take it out the dough will sink or follow
down the place, the dough is ready to
again be turned out on board and shaped
into loaves, and put in pan, let rise in
pan for an hour or an hour and a half, or
until the loaf has risen to almost twice
its original size, it will then be ready
to put in oven to bake, bake in good solid

heat from forty-five to sixty minutes time
depending on size of loaves.

DRY HOP YEAST BREAD

Take one to two yeast cakes, dissolve in
one quart of water of the right
temperature. Now mix in enough flour to
make a medium stiff sponge, let rise until
light or until you can see blubbers come
up and burst, it will then be ready to
make dough, put into this sponge one quart
of water, be sure to get the right
temperature, while adding the water.
Thoroughly mix the
sponge, then add one-half cup sugar,
tablespoon salt, and half cup of soft or
melted lard. Now mix in enough flour to
make a firm dough.

From here on follow the directions for
Home Made Bread as they are the same.

**TO MAKE BREAD WITH COMPRESSED
YEAST**

Take one ounce or ounce and a half, the
amount depending on the kind and strength,
dissolve in one quart of water that is the
right temperature, mix in enough flour to
make a medium stiff sponge, mix well
but do not beat or toughen, let it set
until it has risen and fallen and it can
rise and fall the second time if you so
prefer. It will then be ready to use, add

one quart of water being careful to get it
the right temperature, mix sponge and
water thoroughly, add to the sponge one-
half cup sugar, little more than one
tablespoon salt, half cup soft or melted
lard, mix thoroughly, now mix in enough
flour to make the dough. If hard wheat
flour is used make a soft dough, if soft
wheat flour is used make a stiff dough,
let the dough rise until light then make
into loaves and put in pan, let rise
again, then put in oven and bake.

GRAHAM BREAD

Make sponge of white flour and treat same
as for white bread until it is ready to
make dough. To one quart of sponge add
half cup molasses three tablespoons sugar,
scant tablespoon salt, a little lard and
enough water to make it the right
temperature, mix well, then make dough
using half graham flour and half white
flour.

WHOLE WHEAT BREAD

Follow same directions as for Graham
Bread, but in making the dough use all
whole wheat flour.

RYE BREAD

Make sponge as for white bread, when ready
to make into dough, to each quart of

sponge add half cup sugar, half cup lard,
tablespoon salt, water enough to make it
the right temperature, mix well, then make
dough using half rye and half white flour,
make a stiff dough, and knead it well,
then work off same as for white bread.

SALT RISING BREAD

One of the most important points to be
looked after in baking salt-rising bread
is heat. It must have heat from start to
finish. If you will make a box with
a shelf in it, put the bread on the shelf
and put a pan of hot water under it, and
keep box and all in a warm place, the
steam from the hot water will keep the
dough moist, which will keep a hard crust
from forming on your dough. Put three
teaspoonful of fine cornmeal and a pinch
of soda (about one-twelfth of a
teaspoonful) in a quart bowl. Put one cup
milk and a tablespoonful of water in a
basin and bring to a good, sharp boil.
Pour this on your meal and soda, not too
much at a time, stirring well ail the
time, so it will not be lumpy ; this will
make a very thin batter. Now put your bowl
in a good warm, — not hot, place where the
air cannot strike it and cover it up well
with a cloth to rise. It will take from 12
to 15 hours. The heat must be just warm
but constant. When your yeast is light
take your bowl or vessel, put in one pound
of flour, pour your yeast on the flour,
and stir in with a large spoon. Now add

one and one-fourth pints of water
not scalding, and make a thick batter. Set
this in your box with the hot water under
it, cover it over, keep it good and warm,
but don't get it hot enough to scald.
This will be ready in about an hour,
tablespoon salt, half cup sugar, half cup
lard, one and one-fourth pints hot water
and flour to make a firm dough. Cover up,
set back in box with hot water under it,
let it get a good start in the dough, this
will take twenty to thirty minutes. Turn
out on bread board and work well, shape
into loaves and put in pan. Place in box
with hot water under it, let rise. This
bread must not rise as light as yeast
bread. If it rises too much it will
spoil it. It should never rise enough to
crack on top. The oven should be hot
enough to bake it in twenty to forty
minutes all depending on the size of the
loaf.

ROLLS

In making rolls if you will make them at
the same time you are making bread you
will find it very convenient. You can take
a part of your bread sponge and work into
any kind of roll, coffee cake or raised
doughnuts. If you wish to make rolls and
no bread, make sponge in same manner and
treat same as for bread.

PLAIN ROLLS

To make plain rolls take part of your
bread dough, making it into rolls, put in
pan, setting them a little apart so they
will have room to rise, when risen take a
little cloth and some melted lard and
grease the tops, have the oven hot enough
to bake them in twenty to thirty minutes.

RING ROLLS

Take one quart of sponge add one-half cup
sugar, half cup lard, half a tablespoon
salt, mix well, add about one pint water.
In adding this water get the dough the
temperature you want it, make a stiff
dough and let rise, when light, turn out
on your bread board and take rolling pin
and roll about eight inches wide
and one-fourth inch thick, grease with
melted butter and fold, roll with the
rolling pin a little, and then cut into
strips half inch wide, take strip pull it
a little longer, and at the same time
twisting each end, now pinch the ends
together, it will then be a round ring,
let rise, grease with melted lard and
bake, when baked make a little water icing
(powdered sugar and water) and put a thin
coat on each roll.

TWIST ROLLS

To make twist rolls make dough same as for
ring rolls, roll out the same twist and
lay straight in pan.

CURL ROLLS

Make same dough as for ring rolls, when
dough is light turn out on bread board and
roll out about six or seven inches wide
and one-fourth inch thick, grease with
melted butter and roll up same as jelly
roll, take sharp knife and cut off pieces
about half inch wide, set one cut side
down next to pan, let rise, sprinkle with
sugar and cinnamon and bake.
PARKER HOUSE ROLLS.

Make sponge same as for bread, but make it
with boiled milk that has cooled to the
temperature wanted, when sponge is light.
To each quart of sponge add half cup
sugar, tablespoon salt, half cup butter,
and three eggs, mix well, then mix in
enough flour to make medium stiff dough,
let rise until light. You can make this
dough into any shape you wish. The
following shape is a very good one..

Roll round same as plain rolls, set to one
side and let rise a few minutes. Now take
a knife handle lay it crossways about
center and press down almost mashing the
roll into two pieces, grease with butter
in place made by knife handle, then lay on
side and mash open side together, put in
pan with cut place just a little turned
up, let rise, wash with egg and bake.

GRAHAM ROLLS

Make same as for rolls, using same
ingredients, but in making dough from the
sponge use half graham flour. If you wish
your graham rolls richer add more sugar
and lard.

WHOLE WHEAT ROLLS

Make same as for rolls, using same
ingredients, but in making dough use all
whole wheat flour, if you wish these rolls
richer use more sugar and lard.

COFFEE CAKE

Make sponge same as for bread or rolls,
when sponge is light. To each quart of
sponge add three-fourths cup sugar,
three-fourths cup butter, tablespoon
salt, four eggs or seven yolks, mix well,
then mix in enough flour to make soft
dough, when light turn out
on floured bread board and roll out half
inch thick, put in pan, when light wash
with milk or cream, sprinkle with sugar
and powder with cinnamon. If you like
flavoring you can put in lemon extract to
suit.

To make raisin coffee cake add raisins to
the
above.

DOUGHNUTS WITH YEAST

Make dough same as coffee cake using same
ingredients. But make the dough stiffer,
when light, turn out on well floured bread
board, roll out with rolling pin one-half
inch thick, cut into squares or what ever
shape you wish, or use doughnut cutter,
set in warm place let rise, when light fry
in hot grease, dip in sugar and powder
with cinnamon.

TEA BISCUITS

Six cups of flour.
Four and a half teaspoons baking powder
Three teaspoons salt.
Three ounces lard.
Two and a half cups sweet milk

Sift the flour, baking powder and salt
together, then rub the lard into the
flour, put in the milk and mix into a
light dough. Do not work this dough very
much, you will toughen it, roll out about
half inch thick, cut with round cutter,
set close together in pan, stick with fork
and wash with cream or milk.

BAKING POWDER BISCUITS

One quart flour.
Two rounding tablespoons baking powder.
One tablespoon salt.
One large tablespoon lard.

Sift flour, baking powder and salt

together, mix in lard and pour in enough
cold water or milk to make a soft dough,
mix very light do not toughen by working,
make dough just as soft as you can handle
it, roll out to about half inch thick, cut
with round cutter, put in pan and bake at
once in hot oven.

SODA BISCUITS

One-fourth teaspoon soda.
Two tablespoons baking powder.
Half pound lard.
One and a half pints buttermilk.
Half tablespoon salt.

Add flour enough to make the proper dough.
Take pan biscuits are to be mixed in, sift
in about half the amount of flour, sifting
in the flour at the same time the baking
powder, put in the salt and lard
mix into the flour, dissolve the soda in
part of the milk and add, then add the
rest of the milk, mix, then add enough
flour to make your dough the proper
stiffness, work dough well, working in all
the scraps, lay on well dusted bread board
and roll out until almost half inch thick,
cut with round cutter and bake in hot
oven.

BOSTON BROWN BREAD

Two cupfuls of corn meal.
One cupful of rye meal.
One cupful of graham flour.

One cupful of white flour.
One teaspoon salt.
Two tablespoon baking powder.
One-half cup molasses.
One quart of buttermilk or sour milk.
One-half teaspoon soda.

Put corn meal, rye meal and graham flour
in bowl, put baking powder into white
flour and sift into bowl, add salt and mix
all together, dissolve soda and molasses
in milk, add and mix well, it should be
about the stiffness of muffins. If fresh
milk is used instead of sour milk use more
baking powder and no soda.

Put in well greased deep tins with cover,
fill them almost half full. Set in a pan
with inch and a half water in it, put in
stove, and bake about three and a half
hours, when about half baked, let stove
cool down a little. Or bake in a steamer.

BEATEN BISCUITS

Two pounds flour.
One pint milk, more or less.
Half pound butter.
Tablespoon salt.

Rub the butter in the flour, make a hole,
add the milk with the salt in it and mix.
When mixed beat it out into a medium thin
sheet, fold it over and again beat it out
into a medium thin sheet, repeat this
until the dough is smooth and fine, then
roll it to the thinness you wish your

biscuits to be cut with small round
cutter, dock with docker, or stick with
fork if you have no docker, put in pan and
bake in heat that will bake them thorough,
giving them a nice light brown color, keep
in a dry place, as this biscuit to be good
must be very dry.

Another way is to cut into little squares,
roll round, then mash flat and dock, bake
same as directed above.

SWEET BISCUITS

Two pounds flour.
Half pound lard.
Two tablespoons baking powder.
Half pound sugar
One pint milk.
One teaspoon salt.

Mix and sift together the flour, baking
powder, sugar and salt, then add the milk,
mix up very light but thoroughly, roll out
about half inch thick, cut with round
cutter and bake in hot oven.

CORN MUFFINS

Three-fourths cup sugar.
Three eggs.
Two and a half cups flour.
One and one-half tablespoonful baking
powder.
One-half cupful butter.

Two and one-half cupfuls milk.
 One cupful corn meal.

Cream sugar and butter, cut in the eggs,
add milk and mix well, sift the baking
powder, flour and corn meal together, and
mix in. Fill in well greased moulds and
bake in hot oven.

WHEAT CAKES

Two eggs.
One-half of a teaspoonful of salt.
One tablespoonful of sugar.
One-half cup sweet milk.
One teaspoonful baking powder.
Flour.

Sift together the baking powder sugar,
salt and about half as much flour as you
think it will take, beat up eggs well and
mix in milk, mix all together and
add enough flour to make a soft batter,
heat the griddle iron, grease well and
bake quickly.

DOUGHNUTS WITH BAKING POWDER

One and one-fourth cupfuls granulated
sugar.
One-half cup butter.
Three eggs.
One pint milk.
Four cups flour.
One tablespoonful baking powder.

Cinnamon or lemon flavor.

Whip the sugar, butter and eggs together,
add the milk and flavoring, mix well, sift
the baking powder and flour together and
mix in, roll out to thickness desired, cut
with doughnut cutter and cook in hot
grease, dip in granulated sugar and powder
with cinnamon.

DOUGHNUTS No. 2

One and one-fourth pounds sugar.
Three ounces butter.
One egg.
One-fourth teaspoon salt.
Teaspoonful spices and extract.
One quart milk or water.
Three-fourths ounce baking powder.

Enough flour to make a medium stiff dough.
Follow same directions as for making
doughnuts with baking powder.

DOUGHNUTS No. 3

Your pounds flour.
One-fourth pound butter.
One and one-fourth pound sugar.
3ne quart milk.
Six eggs.
Two and one-half ounces baking powder.

Rub sugar, butter and eggs together add
milk and mix in, then add the flour with

the baking powder sifted in it. Then treat
same as for any other doughnut.

GENERAL REMARKS

Use the very best materials in making
pastry. The flour should be of a good
quality and free from mould or must. The
lard or butter should be good and clean
and if the butter is very salty it should
be washed a little in cold water. The
water used should always be cold, in hot
weather use ice water.

When the crust is made it makes it much
more flaky and brittle if covered with a
cloth and set in a cool place for half
hour or hour, in summer it should be
placed in the ice box.

It improves pie crust to add a little
baking powder. One teaspoonful to a quart
(one pound) of flour is sufficient.

Pie crust can be kept a week or more and
the last will be just as good as the
first, if put in a tightly covered dish,
and set in a cool place in cold weather
and put in the ice box in warm weather,
you can then make fresh pie every day with
little trouble.

Baking pastry requires a good solid heat.
To get a nice bake on your pastry have the

oven hot with a good bed of coals in your
fire box so you can keep your oven at the
right temperature. You can try your oven
and see how hot it is by sprinkling a
little flour in it, if the flour stays
white quite awhile your oven is too cold,
if the flour browns in a little while it
is right, and if it browns quick and then
burns it is too hot.

Pie tins should be greased with good
butter or lard before being used. It adds
very much to the bottom crust if tin is
dusted with cracker meal, always after
dusting turn tin over and knock out the
loose meal.

In making liquid pies such as pumpkin,
custard, etc., or hot fruit pies, it is
much better to bake the bottom crust a
little before putting in the filling.
Always stick the crust in a few places
with a fork before putting it in the oven,
this keeps the steam from forming under it
and raising it up. Baking a little before
filling keeps the crust from being sodden.

If you do not bake the bottom crust always
let the filling cool before putting it in.

PUFF PASTE

One pound of flour, one pound of good
fresh solid butter, two teaspoonfuls
baking powder, one egg, a teaspoonful
salt, a tablespoonful sugar and a cupful

ice water more or less, just enough to
make a medium stiff dough. Half fill a
bowl or pan with cold water. Wash the
butter in this, working it with the hands
until it is light and waxy. This takes out
the salt and buttermilk, and lightens it,
so the pastry is more delicate. Divide the
butter half and half, press out into thin
sheets and put in a pan of cold water to
harden, mix the salt, sugar, baking powder
and flour together, rub into this one
sheet of the butter, whip the egg into a
little of the water and add, then add
enough water to make medium stiff dough.
Sprinkle the board lightly with flour.
Turn the paste on this and roll out
quickly and lightly with the rolling pin.
Do not break the paste. Roll from you, and
to either side. When it is about one-
fourth of an inch thick, take the
remaining butter draining as much of the
water off as possible and breaking it into
little bits spread them over half the
paste sprinkle very lightly with flour.
Fold the paste that has no butter on it
over the butter then fold again and roll
out to about one-third of an inch this
time, fold the dough in from the sides,
not letting the edges touch, then fold in
from the ends and roll again. Repeat this
four times if for pies. But if for
pastries tarts, etc., repeat six times.
Use as little flour as possible while
rolling, excess flour ruins it. Place on
the ice to harden, when it has been rolled
the last time. It should stay on ice at

least an hour before using. In hot weather
if the paste gets sticky while rolling it
out, place on ice a few minutes, as soon
as it gets chilled it will roll much
easier.

PLAIN PUFF PASTE

One pound of flour, one pound of butter,
and ice water enough to make a medium
stiff dough. Rub the butter into the
flour, add the water and mix into dough.
Turn out on dusted board and roll out
until one-fourth inch thick, fold in from
the sides, do not let the edges touch,
then fold in from the ends, fold over
again, set in ice box or cold place for
half hour, then take out and roll out and
fold as before. Repeat and set in ice box
or cool place again for half hour, then
roll out and fold twice more. Then set in
ice box for one hour before using. Do not
use much flour for dusting while rolling.

PATTIES OR SHELLS FOR TARTS

Roll out puff-paste to about one-fourth
inch in thickness, cut out with medium
size cutter, take a smaller cutter and cut
inside the large cutter leaving a ring.
Put in oven and bake. When done take a

small knife and cut the center raised crust out. May be used for oyster or veal patties or filled with jam, jelly or preserves, as tarts. Or if you have patty pans you may line them with puff-paste, they will be fine filled with jam, jelly or preserves, and covered with meringue (one tablespoonful of sugar to the white of one egg well beaten) and browned in oven. If cutters are dipped in hot water the edges will rise higher and be smoother.

JELLY TARTS

Make a good puff paste, roll out very thin, cut into pieces three inches square, wash with well beaten egg, turn the corners in, bake in hot oven, when cool put little squares of jelly in the center.

CREAM TARTS

Line patty tins with a good puff paste and bake, when shells are cool, fill with sweetened whipped cream, lay on the cream a little jelly.

FRUIT TARTS

Line patty shells with puff paste rolled very thin, bake in a hot oven until a light brown, fill the shells with fresh sweetened fruit, cover with sweetened and flavored whipped cream.

CUSTARD TARTS

Line patty pans with best puff paste
rolled out very thin, bake in hot oven
until a delicate brown, then fill with the
following which must be cooked first
Four eggs, two cups milk, tablespoonful
cornstarch, one cupful sugar, two
teaspoonful vanilla, cover with
meringue and brown.

APPLE TARTS

Make shells out of rich puff paste and
fill with the following, which must be
cooked first. Two cups apple sauce, two
eggs, one cupful rich cream, juice of one
lemon, one and one-fourth cupful
granulated sugar. Make meringue to go on
top and brown.

PLAIN PIE CRUST

Rub into one pound of flour half pound of
lard, add a pinch of salt, add enough cold
water to make a soft dough, work just as
little as possible.

GOOD PIE CRUST

Rub into one pound of flour four ounces of
lard and four ounces of good butter, add a
pinch of salt, add enough cold water to

make a soft dough, do not work it any more
than to get it mixed, the dough should be
just as soft as you can handle it.

RICH PIE CRUST

Sift one teaspoonful baking powder in one
pound of flour, rub into this eight ounces
of good butter, add a pinch of salt, add
enough cold water to make a soft dough, do
not work, mix it just as light as you can,
just so there is no dry flour left, put in
ice box or cold place and let set for an
hour or more, it will then be ready to
use.

HOW TO MAKE A PIE

After making the pie dough take a portion
of it and lay on well dusted board, dust
the dough on top just a little, take
rolling pin and rub a little flour on it,
make two rolls side ways, then dust the
dough again if sticky, then proceed by
rolling to and from you, roll until the
crust is the thinness desired, about one-
eighth inch is about right. Rolling out
the crust this way you do not have to turn
it over and over, which ruins crust to a
certain extent, when not turned it makes
it flaky and crisp. Now fit the rolled out
dough to the pie pan, cut the edge all the
way around, take dough cut off and some
fresh dough and roll as before, the top
crust should be a little thinner than the

bottom, when rolled to thinness desired, fold over until it looks like a half crust, take a sharp knife and cut several places along the doubled edge, this is for the steam to escape. Now fill your pie plate with your filling, lay top crust on pie and turn back the lapel part of the crust press around the rim sealing the two crusts, take a fork and mark around the edge, dipping the fork in flour occasionally to prevent sticking, brush the loose flour off the top and bake in rather a quick oven until a light brown, and the filling boils up through the cut places in the crust.

If you wish a gloss on your pie wash the top with an egg before baking.

HOW TO PREPARE FILLINGS FOR PIES

Never soak any pie filling over night. Dried or evaporated fruit such as peaches, apricots or apples should be cooked until swelled. About one quart of water to half pound of fruit. When fruit is cooked tender stir in about cup and a half granulated sugar. Amount of sugar depending on the sourness of the fruit, add a pinch of salt.

It improves fresh berry pies to mix the berries with sugar and let stand over night, then drain the juice off and boil adding a little corn starch, pour this

back on the berries, they will then be
ready for pie.

LEMON PIE No. 1

Boil half cup apples and one cup sugar in
one and one-half cupful of water until
apples are soft. Dissolve two
tablespoonful cornstarch in a little cold
water, stir into cooked apples while
cooking, remove from the stove and when
cool add two eggs, pinch of salt, juice
and grated rind of one lemon, and
teaspoonful good butter. Run through
colander and fill pie pans lined with your
pie crust, bake in hot oven, when
baked, beat the whites of two eggs adding
two tablespoonful sugar, spread over top
and set back in oven until brown.

LEMON PIE No. 2

Squeeze out the juice of two lemons, and
grate the rind in a deep dish, add a cup
and a half of granulated sugar and two
tablespoonful flour, or one of cornstarch,
and mix, add the yolks of three eggs
(saving the whites) juice of lemons and a
small table spoonful butter, whip up
thoroughly, add two cups water and mix,
set this into another dish containing
water and boil until it thickens. Remove
it from the fire and when cool, pour it
into deep pie tin lined with your pie

crust, bake, and when done have the whites
beaten stiff with two heaping
tablespoonful sugar, spread this over the
top, return to the oven and let brown.

LEMON PIE No. 3

One cupful of sugar, the yolks of three
eggs, one tablespoonful soft or melted
butter, one heaping table- spoonful of
flour or one heaping teaspoonful of cornstarch, and the juice and a little of the
rind grated, whip this up thoroughly, then
add one cupful water and mix. Put in pie
tin lined with your pie dough and bake
thirty-five or forty minutes, when baked
have the egg whites beaten stiff with a
tablespoonful sugar added, spread over the
top and return to the oven and let brown.

If the above filling is boiled in a double
boiler a little before putting in pie
crust it will be some better.

LEMON PIE No. 4

Grate the rind and use the juice of one
lemon, add three-fourths of a cup of
sugar, a tablespoonful of melt- ed butter,
and the yolks of two eggs, whip this up
thoroughly, then add a scant pint of milk
with two tablespoonful of cornstarch
dissolved in it. Put in pie tin lined with
pie dough and bake, when baked have the
whites of the eggs well beaten with two
tablespoonful sugar added, spread on top

of pie and return to oven and brown.

COOKED GREEN APPLE PIE

Take as many apples as you wish for your pies, peel and core them, also cut out all defective and rotten places, put in dish, add a little water and put on stove and let cook, when soft sweeten to taste, let cook just a little longer stirring them well then let cool, when cool flavor with lemon or lemon juice, cinnamon or nutmeg, line pie tin with your pie dough and bake in solid heat until a light brown.

CANNED APPLE No. 1

Take the apples out of the can, pour off the liquor, and chop up the apples, sweeten to taste, add table-spoonful melted butter, flavor with nutmeg, cinnamon or the juice of one lemon, line pie pan with your pie crust, put in the filling, put on top crust and bake in hot oven until a light brown.

CANNED APPLE No. 2

Take the apples out of the can, put the juice in dish and apples in another, chop up the apples adding one-half cup of granulated sugar to each pie. Put the juice On the stove and let come to a boil. Dissolve a little cornstarch in cold water and stir in enough to make it a little

thick, add the juice of half a lemon, or
flavor with cinnamon or nutmeg, stir well
then, mix into the chopped apples.
Line a pie pan with your pie crust and
fill, put on top crust. Top crust must
have several places cut in
it to let the steam escape. Bake in hot
oven until a light brown.

APPLE MERINGUE

Take two cups of cooked apples, dried,
canned or fresh, mix in one cup sugar more
or less, amount of sugar depending on the
sourness of the apples, stir in
the juice of half a lemon, beat the whites
of two or three eggs stiff, adding a pinch
of salt. Now mix the egg whites into the
apples, (the apple must be cool). Line pie
pan with your pie dough and fill, for top
crust lay strips one inch wide and one
inch apart across the pie, then lay more
strips across the other way, forming a
sort of checker board. Put in oven and
bake a light brown.

If preferred the egg white can be put on
top and not mixed in, but in this case the
pie must first be baked, then the white
put on and browned.

SLICED APPLE PIE

Take good sound apples, peel, quarter, and
cut out the core, then slice into thin,
slices. Line your pie pan with your pie

dough, fill with the sliced apple, sprinkle over the apples half cup granulated sugar, more or less amount of sugar depending on sourness of apples. Scatter little pieces of butter over it and flavor with the juice of half a lemon, cinnamon or nutmeg, sprinkle with a little flour. For top roll out your dough and cut into strip one inch wide and long enough to reach across the pie, lay across the pie about an inch apart, then lay strips cross the other way in like manner. Put in oven and bake until a light brown, and the apples are done.

APPLE CUSTARD PIE

Take one cupful of well cooked dried, fresh or canned apples, mash and rub through colander, add half cup granulated sugar, more or less, amount depending on the sourness of the apples. Now mix the yolks of two eggs, three tablespoonful sugar, one heaping tablespoonful of cornstarch or two of flour, one pint of milk and a pinch of salt, whip this well, then set on stove and let it come to a boil, then add apples and mix, take off and let cool, when cool put in pie pan, lined with your pie dough and bake, when baked have the whites of the eggs whipped stiff with two tablespoonful sugar added, spread on pie and return to oven and let brown.

This can be made without boiling the

custard.

PLAIN CHERRY PIE

Wash and seed enough cherries for one pie,
to each cup of cherries take three-fourths
cupful sugar more or less, amount of sugar
depending on the sourness of your
cherries, line pie pan with your pie dough
and fill, sprinkle a little flour over the
cherries, put on top crust and bake in hot
oven until a light brown and until the
filling boils up through holes in crust.

CHERRY CUSTARD PIE

Line a pie plate with your pie dough, lay
enough cherries in bottom to make about
one-third of the thickness of the pie.
Make a custard of the following:
Yolks of two eggs, three tablespoonful
sugar, one tablespoonful cornstarch or two
of flour, one cup of milk and a pinch of
salt, whip this, thoroughly mixing it,
pour on cherries and put in stove and
bake, when baked have ready the whites
beaten stiff with two tablespoonful sugar
added, spread on top and return to oven
and brown.

BEST CHERRY PIE

Line a pie tin with your pie dough and put
in enough washed and seeded cherries to
make about one- third the thickness of the
pie, dissolve one ounce of gelatin in one

pint of water, add two tablespoonful
of granulated sugar, mix well, pour over
the cherries and bake, when done let cool
a little. Then have ready the whites of
two or three eggs whipped stiff with two
tablespoonful of sugar and a pinch of salt
added. Let pie cool a little and spread
the whites on it and return to oven and
brown.

RAISIN PIE

Stir and wash two cups raisins, put them
into a stew pan, with one and one-fourth
cupfuls cold water and three-fourths
cupful sugar. Cover tight and let
come to a boil, then simmer for fifteen or
twenty minutes. Make a smooth paste of
some flour and cold water, pour in enough
to thicken a little, must stir constantly
while pouring in the paste, or it will be
lumpy, add a tablespoonful butter and a
teaspoonful lemon extract. When cool bake
between two crusts in a hot oven until a
light brown.

PLUM OR DAMSON PIE

Use good ripe plums or damsons, wash
thoroughly. Line a deep pie tin with a
rich crust, fill with the damsons or
plums, if they are free stone damsons
they should be seeded, sprinkle over them
enough granulated sugar to sweeten them,
then sprinkle over the sugar one
tablespoonful flour, put a small piece of

butter in, put on top crust and bake in a
moderate oven until a light brown and the
filling boils up through the cut places in
the crust.

TRANSPARENT PIE

Two cups sugar.
One-half cupful butter.
One and one-half cupfuls cream.
Six eggs.
Half teaspoonful vanilla.

The above is enough for two pies, cream
the sugar and butter, beat the yolks and
whites of the eggs separately, whip in the
yolks, leave out enough of the whites for
the top, add rest and mix, add the cream
and mix, add the flavoring and mix. Line a
deep dish with a good crust and bake in a
moderate oven until a delicate brown. When
done take the remaining egg whites, add
sugar and flavoring, spread on top, return
to the oven and brown.

CUSTARD PIE

Yolks of two eggs, save whites.
Three tablespoonful sugar.
One and half tablespoonful cornstarch.
One heaping tablespoonful flour.
One pint milk.
One pinch salt.

Mix together and whip thoroughly, put in
pie plate lined with pie crust, bake in
hot oven, when done have ready the whites

beaten stiff with two table- spoonful
sugar and a pinch of salt added, spread
over pie and return to oven and brown.

CREAM PIE

Three cups cream.
Three tablespoonful cornstarch.
Yolks of three eggs.
One tablespoonful lemon extract.

Take cream, cornstarch and yolks and whip
together, then put on stove and boil until
it thickens, take off stove and stir in
lemons. Line pie tin with your
pie dough and bake in oven, stick pie
dough with fork before baking, this will
let the steam from under it, keeping the
crust from raising up, put in filling and
bake, when baked have ready the whites
beaten stiff with half cup sugar added,
spread on top and return to
oven and brown.

CREAM PIE No. 2

Three cups milk.
Two eggs.
Three tablespoonful cornstarch
One teaspoon lemon or orange extract.

Whip together the eggs, milk, extract and
corn starch until smooth. Put in pie tin
lined with your pie dough and bake in hot

oven.

COCONUT PIE

Yolks of three eggs.
Three tablespoonful of sugar.
One tablespoonful cornstarch.
Half cup of granulated coconut.

Whip together the eggs, cornstarch and
sugar, and add the cocoanut, put in pie
tin lined with plain pie crust and bake,
when baked have ready the whites
beaten stiff with half cup sugar added,
spread over top and return to oven and
brown.

PLAIN CHOCOLATE PIE

One-fourth of a cupful grated chocolate,
one pint of water, yolks of two eggs,
(save the whites) two tablespoonful
cornstarch or four of flour, half cupful
of sugar, and teaspoonful vanilla,
dissolve the chocolate in part of the
water by putting it on the back of
the stove and let simmer, add the rest of
the water, yolks, cornstarch, and sugar,
whip all together, put on stove and boil
until it thickens, add vanilla. Line pie
plate with your pie dough, set another pan
the same size in it and bake, when half

done, take pan out, and bake done, then
pour in filling, whip the whites of the
eggs stiff, add two tablespoonful of
sugar, spread on top and set in oven and
let brown.

BEST CHOCOLATT PIE

Take one-third of a cupful chocolate,
grated; one pint of milk, one-third of a
cup sugar, three eggs, and one teaspoonful
vanilla. Dissolve the chocolate in a
little of the milk, whip up the eggs and
sugar in the rest of the milk, pour in
when chocolate is dissolved. Put on stove
and 1-et boil for three minutes. Line pie
tin with your pie dough and hake, the
dough should be stuck with a fork, or
another pan the same size set in it, to
keep crust from raising up, when done pour
in the filling, let cool a little, then
beat the whites of two eggs stiff with two
tablespoonful sugar added, spread on to
top, dust with sugar, set in oven and
brown.

PLAIN RHUBARB PIE

Cut the leaf off the stem and pull the
skin off, cut into small pieces. Line pie
pan with your pie crust and fill with the
rhubarb, to each cupful of rhubarb take
half cup sugar, sprinkle this on the
rhubarb, sprinkle with a little flour or
cornstarch, put on top crust, then put in

oven and bake until the crust is a light
brown, and the rhubarb is cooked done.

GOOD RHUBARB PIE

Cut the ends off the stern and peel the
skin off, cut into small pieces, to each
cupful of rhubarb take half cup sugar, put
sugar on rhubarb and let set over
night, next morning strain the juice off
and set on the stove and cook, when
boiling add the rhubarb and cook until
tender, dissolve a little cornstarch or
flour in cold water, and pour in enough to
thicken a little. Line pie pan with your
pie dough and put in the filling (the
filling should be cooled before going in
crust) put on top crust and bake in hot
oven until the crust is a light brown.

BEST RHUBARB PIES

Cut the ends of the stalk and pull the
skin off, cut into small pieces, cover
well with sugar and let set over night,
next morning drain the juice off and put
on stove and cook, when it comes to a boil
add the rhubarb, cook until tender, take
off stove and let cool, when cool add one
or two eggs, half cup cracker meal and
pinch of salt to each pie, mix all
together. Line pie pan with your pie
crust, fill, put on top crust and bake in
a hot oven until a light brown.

PLAIN GOOSEBERRY PIE

Stem and wash as many gooseberries as you
think it will take for your pie, for each
cupful of gooseberries take half cupful
sugar, or more, amount of sugar depending
on ripeness of berries. Line your pie pan
with pie dough and fill with berries,
sprinkle the sugar over them, then
sprinkle some flour or cornstarch
over the sugar, put on your top crust, be
sure and make the bottom and top crust
stick together around the edge, and cut a
number of holes in the top crust, bake in
hot oven until a light brown.

BEST GOOSEBERRY PIE

Take enough gooseberries for one pie, stem
and wash them, for each cup of
gooseberries take half cupful sugar, add
just a little water to start them to cook,
put on stove and cook until done, let
cool, when cooled mix in one egg and half
cupful cracker meal to each pie. Line pie
pan with pie dough and fill with the
filling, put on the top crust and bake in
hot oven until a light brown.

ORANGE PIE

Grate the rind and use the juice of one
large or two small oranges, add to this
one-half cupful sugar, the well beaten
yolks of two or three eggs, (saving the
whites for frosting), one tablespoonful

flour, or one and one-half teaspoonful
cornstarch, tablespoonful melted butter,
and one cup water, mix all together
thoroughly. Line pie pan with pie crust
and fill, bake in a hot oven until filling
gets thick, when done, have ready the
whites beaten stiff with three tablespoonful sugar mixed in, spread on top,
sprinkle with sugar and put in oven and
brown.

FRESH CURRANT PIE

Stem and wash the currants, then mash, to
each cup of mashed currants add one cupful
granulated sugar and one well beaten egg.
Line pie pan with pie dough and fill, put
several little pieces of butter over the
filling, put on top crust and bake in hot
oven until a light brown and until the
filling boils up through the holes in
crust. If the currants are very green they
should be cooked a little before going
into the pie.

DRIED APRICOT

Wash and pick over the dried apricots, put
in pan, add a little water and cook until
soft, when soft sweeten to taste stirring
in the sugar, then let cool. Line pie pan
with plain pie crust, fill, put on top
crust and bake a light brown.

DRIED APRICOT No. 2

Wash and pick over the dried apricots, put
in pan, add a little water and cook until
very soft, run through colander, sweeten
to taste. Line pie tin with plain pie
dough, fill, put several little pieces of
butter over the top, cover, and bake a
light brown.

FRESH APRICOT

Cut out the bad places, and cut off the
seed and wash. Line pie pan with plain pie
crust and fill, sprinkle over with three-
fourths cupful granulated sugar, more or
less amount depending on the sourness
of the fruit and the size of the pie,
sprinkle a little flour or cornstarch over
the sugar, and put several little pieces
of butter over it, cover with top crust
and bake in hot oven until the crust is a
light brown and the filling boils up
through the holes in crust.

APPLE APRICOT PIE

Apricots are so rich that they do not make
an extra good pie. Take half enough fresh
or dried apricots and half enough fresh or
dried apples, put them in a pan, add a
little water, boil until soft, then run
through a colander, sweeten to taste and
let cool. Line pie dish with pie dough and
fill, put a tablespoonful melted butter

over the filling, sprinkle with a little
cinnamon. Put on top crust and bake a
light brown.

BLACKBERRY PIE

The blackberries should be picked over and
washed, drain all the water off. To each
cupful of blackberries take half cupful
sugar more or less, amount depending on
sourness and ripeness of the berries. Line
pie tin with plain pie dough and fill,
put several little pieces of butter on,,
then put on top crust and bake until a
light brown and the filling boils up
through the holes in the crust.

DEW BERRY PIE

Make same as for blackberry pie.

FRESH PEACH PIE

Peel enough peaches and slice into thin
slices, to each cup of sliced peaches add
half cup sugar. Line
pie pan with pie dough and fill, put
tablespoonful melted butter over the
peaches and sugar. Put on top crust and
bake a light brown and until the fruit
boils up through the holes in the crust.

CANNED PEACHES

Chop the peaches up fine, sweeten to

taste, fill pie pan lined with pie crust,
flavor with a little butter. Put on top
crust and bake in hot oven.

PLAIN DRIED PEACH PIE

Pick over and wash the dried peaches, add
a little water and cook until soft, stir
in enough sugar to sweeten, let cool. Line
pie tin and fill, bake in hot oven.

GOOD DRIED PEACH PIE

Pick over and thoroughly wash the peaches
for your pies, add a little water and cook
until very soft, then run through a
colander, for each cupful peaches
take almost half cupful sugar stir
together, fill pie tin lined with dough
put tablespoonful butter over top, of
filling, put on top crust and bake in hot
oven.

PLAIN PUMPKIN PIE.

One pint of fresh cooked or canned
pumpkin.
One and one-half cupfuls sugar.
Two tablespoonful Flour.
Four eggs.
One pint milk.
Cinnamon, ginger and salt to taste.

Mix the pumpkin, sugar, flour and egg
together, whip this up well, add the
cinnamon, ginger and salt and mix, add the
milk little at a time, stirring it in,
when milk is all in. Line pie tin with
puff paste or pie dough, fill with the
filling and bake in a hot oven.

GOOD PUMPKIN PIE

Peel the pumpkin cut into small pieces,
add a little water and boil until very
soft, mash with rum through colander, or
use canned pumpkin.
Dint of pumpkin add the following:

One-half cupful sugar.
Half cupful good molasses.
Two eggs.
Two teaspoonful cinnamon.
Two teaspoonful ginger.
One teaspoonful salt.
One tablespoonful flour.
One cupful milk.

Mix pumpkin, sugar, molasses cinnamon,
ginger, salt and flour, whipping them
well, beat eggs, add and mix y add the
milk and mix. Line deep pie tin with puff
paste or pie dough, put in the filling and
bake in a hot oven until a light brown.

BEST PUMPKIN PIE

Take the whole pumpkin, put in pan and set
in oven and let bake four to five hours,

when done cut the pumpkin open, scrape out
the seeds, then scrape out the meat in a
dish, run this through a colander. Get
one pint of pumpkin add the following:

One cupful sugar.
Half cup best molasses.
Four eggs.
One and one-half cupful thick sweet cream
Three teaspoonful ginger.
One teaspoonful cinnamon.
One-half teaspoonful salt.
Two teaspoonful cornstarch.

To the pumpkin add the sugar, molasses,
ginger, cinnamon and salt, dissolve the
cornstarch in the cream, then add and
thoroughly mix, beat the yolks and whites
of the eggs separately, add the yolks and
mix, then add the whites stir in lightly.
Line deep pie pan with puff paste or best
pie crust, fill and bake in a hot oven
until a light brown. Then cover top
with whipped cream sweetened a little.

SWEET POTATO PIE

One and one-half cup boiled and pulped
sweet potatoes.
One and one-half cupfuls milk.
Three-fourths cup sugar.
One-half teaspoonful lemon or two
tablespoonful brandy.
Yolks of two eggs (save whites.)

Mix the potato, milk, sugar, eggs, salt

and flavoring all together. Line a pie tin
with a rich pie dough and bake in a hot
oven until a light brown. Beat the
whites stiff, adding tablespoonful sugar,
spread on top and return to oven and
brown.

SLICED SWEET POTATO PIE

Peel the potatoes and bake, when cool
slice in small slices into a deep pan
lined with a good crusty lay a layer of
slices, sprinkle with sugar, repeat until
pie is filled, put two tablespoonful
melted butter in, pour in a little milk or
cream, put on top crust and bake in hot
oven to a light brown.

PLUM PUDDING

One pound sugar
One pound raisins
One pound currants
One-half pound citron and orange peel
One pound suet chopped fine
Five eggs.
Three teaspoonful soda.
Three teaspoonful cinnamon.
Two teaspoonful salt.
One pint water.

Flour enough to make medium soft dough
Mix all together, put in sack and boil for
five hours. Let set in cool dry place for
one month. When you want to use it heat
and serve with wine or brandy sauce.

PEACH DUMPLING

Take good, fresh, ripe fruit, wash and peel, cut into halves, taking seed out. Make a good rich puff paste and roll out one-fourth inch thick, cut into squares large enough to cover a peach. Take two halves of the peaches and put together, fill the hole left by the seed with granulated sugar, and put a small piece of butter on top, set in the center of the square piece of puff paste, take the corners and fold over, making a ball, set in pan smooth side up, bake in moderate oven until a nice brown. Serve with whipped cream or cream sauce.

APPLE DUMPLING

Take good sound ripe apples, wash, peel and cut the core out with a core cutter. Make a good puff paste or pie dough and roll out to one-fourth inch thick, cut in squares large enough to cover the apple. Wash squares of dough with egg, set apple in center of dough, fill hole in center with sugar, put a piece of butter on top, flavor with cinnamon, nutmeg or juice of lemon, take corners of dough and fold over the apple making a ball, set in pan with folded side down. Bake in moderate oven until a light brown. Serve with sweetened whipped cream or cream sauce.

FRUIT ROLL

Take any kind of pie fruit that is not too juicy. Make puff paste or a good pie dough, roil out to one fourth inch thick, spread the filling all over it, except about an inch around the edge, roll up same as jelly roll, seal the ends and lay in pan with the joined side down, bake in moderate oven until a nice brown, cut into slices and serve with sweetened whipped cream, or the following sauce: One cup water, one tea- spoonful cornstarch, two tablespoonful melted butter, half cupful sugar, lemon flavoring, mix the corn- starch and water, add the rest and cook.

GENERAL DIRECTIONS

As so much depends on good ingredients in cake making, each ingredient will be dealt with separately.

Flour

Flour is one of the most important ingredients used in cake making, so much depends on the flour that it is absolutely necessary to have the best if you wish your goods to be first class.

The best flour for cake making is soft wheat, also called pastry flour, this flour is ground fine, and is especially adapted to cake making. You can make cake

from hard wheat flour but you must learn
how to use it, as a general thing you
should use a little less, much depending
on the strength and milling of it. As
there are so many brands of this kind of
flour it is impossible to give a rule that
will suit all. The only way is to buy a
good brand, learn how to use it and stick
to it.

Flour should always be kept in a dry
place, before using: it for cake, it
should be well dried out, but never mix
warm flour into cake, it should always be
cool. Always sift the flour before using
it.

Butter

Butter is another important ingredient, it
should always be thoroughly washed in
several waters, the waters always being
cold enough to keep the butter firm.
Washing takes out the salt and buttermilk
and makes it fresher thereby making it
easier to cream.

It is hard to make good cake, using butter
that has butter coloring in it. It won't
cream white. Margarine is not a good
substitute for butter in cake, but if you
have to use it always use less than the
recipe calls for. Cottolene comes nearer
filling the place of good butter than

anything else. But in using it only use
about three-fourths as much as the recipe
calls for butter if a recipe calls for one
pound butter use twelve ounces cottolene.
If your butter is strong use more
flavoring.

Sugar

Any good grade of sugar will give good
results, but for best results and ease of
working use powdered sugar.

Flavoring and Baking Powder

There are so many different brands of
flavoring and baking powder, that it is
impossible to tell just how much to use,
buy a good brand and learn to use it, and
stick to it, and if the amount given in
the recipe, in your judgment is not enough
or is too much change to suit yourself.

Eggs

Eggs should be fresh if you wish good
flavored and good looking fine grained
cake. Eggs should always be beaten up
cold, in whipping the air into the
egg if it is warm the walls of the air
cells are weak and they soon break
returning to liquid again, they are
then hard to beat up again, but when they
are cold it makes the air cells strong and
once whipped up they stay, provided
nothing warm is mixed in with them,

therefore you can see that it is very
necessary to have the other ingredients a
little cool.

For many years it has been customary to
beat the yolks and whites separately, and
many of the recipes in this book contain
this in its instructions accompanying
the recipe, this is done simply because it
has been the custom. It is now being
argued by many of the best workman in the
baking trade that finer cake is made
where the butter and sugar is creamed and
the eggs are added one or two at a time
and either whipped in with a good strong
egg whip or creamed in with the hand. It
is recommended that you try both ways and
see for yourself which is the better way,
this applies to where whole eggs are used.
Where whites only are used they should be
whipped stiff. A pinch of salt or soda
added to eggs makes them beat easier. And
always whip the same direction.

Other Materials

Soda should always be dissolved in a
little water or milk. Baking powder and
cream of tartar should be sifted with the
flour.

All fruit such as raisins, currants, figs,
etc., should be carefully picked over, and
washed if necessary, then dried on a cloth
near the fire. If not well dried the cake

in which you put them will be heavy. Fruit
should be rubbed in flour and the surplus
flour shook off.

Use ground spices or pulverize them.
How Moulds and Tins Should be Prepared.
Cake pans should be thoroughly cleaned and
greased, unsalted butter is the best, let
a little butter melt the salt will sink to
the bottom, large pans should be lined
with paper which should also be well
greased, if the mould is not large enough
you can let the paper extend above the
mould, at least two thicknesses should be
placed in the bottom, layer cake tins
should be well greased then dusted with
flour, then turned over and all surplus
flour jarred out.

The Oven and How to Bake

The oven should be moderately hot, it
should be heated up before the cake is
ready to go in. One way to tell if the
oven is right is to put a small spoon of
flour in the oven if this turns a nice
brown in about five minutes the oven is
alright, another way is to try it with a
little of the dough. Do not* open the oven
door often when bake is in the oven the
cold air won't do it any good, if the oven
is too hot put a paper over the cake and
try and regulate your fire. Be very

careful not to jar the cake while baking,
it will fall Ft you do. The best and
easiest way to tell when the cake is done
is to stick a broom straw in it if the
straw comes out clean the cake is done.
You can tell when layer and small cookies
or cakes are done by pressing the finger
down on them just a little if the cake
raises back not leaving the impression
made, the cake is done, but if the
impression stays there the cake must bake
longer. Cakes with molasses or fruit in
them do not need as much heat.

Mixing Cake

Never stir around after the butter and
sugar are creamed, always mix from the
bottom up and lap it over, this laps air
into the cake dough and produces little
air cells, which causes the dough to puff
and swell when it comes in contact with
the heat while baking.

It takes work and experience to make good
cake, if you will learn to do three things
you will have no trouble, they are select
good materials, cream and mix
properly and be careful in baking.

CHRISTMAS FRUIT CAKE

One pound good butter.
One pound powdered sugar.
One pound flour.
One pound currants, cleaned and dried.

Twelve eggs.
Heaping teaspoonful each of ground ginger,
cinnamon and mixed spices.
Lemon flavoring.
One pound mixed citron, lemon and orange
peel.
Half pound figs cut fine.
Half pound dried cherries.
One pound raisins, stoned (pitted).

Cream the butter and sugar, beat the
whites and yolks separately, and add to
the creamed butter and sugar, add next the
cinnamon, ginger, spices and flavoring,
mix thoroughly, put the fruit in the flour
and mix, then add, mixing in very lightly
but thoroughly, grease mould and line with
two or three thicknesses of paper greasing
the paper with unsalted butter, bake in a
slow oven until done, decorate to suit
yourself.

LARGE FRUIT CAKE

Two pounds good butter.
Two pounds powdered sugar.
Two and one-fourth pounds flour.
Eighteen eggs.
One-fourth pound each of citron, lemon and
orange peel.
One pound chopped almonds.
Tablespoonful good mixed spices.
Two pounds of seedless or stoned (pitted)
raisins chopped.

One pound chopped figs.
Teaspoonful ground ginger.
One-fourth pound cleaned currants.
One teaspoonful lemon extract.

Cream the butter and sugar, put the eggs
in two at a time, thoroughly whipping them
in with a good stiff egg whip, add the
ground ginger, lemon extract and mixed
spices, and mix thoroughly, add the
chopped peel and the chopped almonds and
mix, (the almonds should be skinned,
soaking them a few minutes in hot
water will make the skin slip off easy,
then brown in the oven, when cool chop.)
The fruit should be drenched in the flour
and the flour shook off as much as
possible, add the fruit and mix, then add
the flour, and mix in very lightly but
thoroughly. Line mould with several
thicknesses of paper well greased with
unsalted butter. This cake should be baked
in a slow heat, a cake seven to nine
pounds in weight, will take four and a
half to six hours to bake according to the
heat. When done ice and decorate in any
style you may wish.

LITTLE FRUIT CAKE.

One pound, two ounces flour.
One pound good firm butter.
One pound powdered sugar.
Ten eggs.
Half pound currants.
Half pound chopped figs.

One and one-fourth pounds seedless or
stoned (pitted)
raisins chopped.
Half pound blanched almonds chopped.
Half pound mixed citron, lemon and orange
peels.
Half teaspoonful nutmeg grated,
Two tablespoonful mixed spices.
Two teaspoonful ground ginger.
Teaspoonful extract of lemon.

Mix according to the directions of Large
Fruit cake.

FRUIT CAKE

Two pounds flour.
One pound butter.
Five pounds of raisins, currants, dried
cherries.
One pound chopped nuts.
One tablespoonful ground cloves.
Two tablespoonful ground cinnamon.
Two pounds powdered sugar.
Sixteen eggs.
Lemon flavor.

Cream the butter and sugar, dropping in
the eggs a few at a time and whipping
well, drench the fruit in the flour, take
out and mix, add the flavoring extract
and spices, mix well, then add the flour.
Line mould with heavy paper, grease both
mould and paper, fill and bake in slow
oven.

BIRTHDAY FRUIT CAKE

One pound good butter.
One pound, two ounces of flour.
One pound of sultana raisins.
One teaspoonful good mixed spices.
Half pound each of sliced citron, orange
and lemon peels.
One pound sugar.
Ten eggs.
One-half pound blanched almonds chopped.
One teaspoonful ground ginger.
One cupful cleaned currants.

Cream the butter, eggs and sugar, adding
the ginger and spices while creaming, when
creamed, add the flour and half mix; then
add all but the currants, mixlightly but
thoroughly, when about mixed add the currants. When mixed put it into a round cake
tin, which has been well prepared side and
bottom, let the paper stand up an inch
above the tin, smooth the mixture level
and bake in a slow heat. It will take
about four hours to bake this cake. When
half baked put a sheet of paper over it,
this is to keep it from getting too much
color. When you think it is baked draw it
gently to the front and stick a broom
straw or wire in it, then take it out, if
it comes out clean and smooth the
cake is baked, if any of the mixture
sticks it shows the cake is not fully
baked, return to the oven as gently as
possible. When baked, let cool, pull off
the paper, and cut off the rough places

with a sharp knife and ice.

ALMOND FRUIT CAKE

One pound butter.
One pound sugar.
One and one-half pounds flour.
Ten eggs.
One-half pound chopped figs.
One pound of stoned or seedless raisins.

Cream the butter and sugar, add the eggs
two at a time, whipping them in with a
good egg whip, drench the fruit in the
flour, take fruit out of flour, shaking
off all loose flour and mix in, sift the
flour and baking powder together, mix in
lightly but thoroughly, fill mould and
cover top with split almonds, bake.

ANGEL FOOD

Fourteen ounces flour.
Fourteen ounces powdered sugar.
Three-fourths teaspoonful cream of tartar.
Whites of twenty-four eggs.
Flavoring, any kind.
Sift the flour and cream of tartar
together six to ten times, whip the eggs
very stiff, when stiff add the sugar a
little at a time and thoroughly whip in,
then add the flavoring, add the flour and
fully but lightly mix it in. Bake in the
regular angel food cake tins. The tins for

this must be well cleaned and free from
any roughness, and must not be greased,
fill so the pan will be almost full when
baked. When baked turn upside down, if
cake does not drop out by the time it is
cold take knife and run around the edge
and give a gentle shake.

ANGEL FOOD

One pound powdered sugar.
One pound flour.
Whites of twenty eggs.
Half ounce cream of tartar.
Two teaspoonful vanilla.

Beat the egg whites very stiff, add the
flavoring and thoroughly whip in, sift the
sugar, flour and cream of tartar eight
times and mix in fully but lightly, fill
your prepared moulds and bake in a
moderate oven. When cold brush off the
crumbs and ice with any good icing, and
color to suit yourself.

ANGEL CAKE

One and one-half cups granulated sugar.
One cupful flour.
Whites of eleven eggs.
Two teaspoonful vanilla.
One even teaspoonful cream of tartar.

Sift the sugar, flour and cream of tartar
eight to ten times, beat the white of eggs
very stiff, adding a pinch of salt to them
before commencing, mix the flavoring into
the eggs, then mix the flour in, mixing
fully but lightly. Do not whip the flour
in. Do not grease the moulds, they should
be clean and free from grease. Fill your
mould and bake in moderate oven, when cold
ice with a good icing.

POUND CAKE

Six eggs.
One pound sugar.
One pound butter.
One pound, four ounces flour.
One tablespoonful baking powder.
One cup milk.

Cream the sugar and butter, add the milk,
mixing well, sift the baking powder and
flour together at least five times, add,
mix in very lightly, add flavoring, beat
eggs very light, add yolks first and mix
in lightly, then add whites and mix in
very lightly, put in mould, grease and
lined with paper greased, and bake.

POUND CAKE No. 2

Eleven eggs.
One and one-fourth pounds flour.
One pound of good butter.
One pound of sugar.

One tablespoonful baking powder.
Two teaspoonful lemon or vanilla extract.

Cream the butter and sugar if you have it
or can get it, use pulverized sugar, it
will work easier and quicker, beat the
eggs separately and add, sift the baking
powder in the flour, at least four times,
add and mix in very lightly, add flavoring
and mix lightly. Grease mould and line
with paper, grease paper with unsalted
butter, bake in a moderate heat until
done.

POUND CAKE No. 3

One pound flour.
One pound sugar.
One pound butter.
Ten eggs.
Two teaspoonful baking powder.
Two teaspoonful vanilla.
Cream the butter and sugar.

Beat the eggs separately and add one or
two at a time and whip in with a good
strong egg whip, sift the baking powder
with the flour four times, put in and mix
lightly, add flavoring and mix lightly,
bake in moderate oven from one hour and a
half to two and a half, length depending
on heat of oven.

LADY CAKE

Three-fourths pound sugar.
Half pound butter.
One pound flour.
Ten egg whites.
Teaspoonful vanilla.
Two teaspoonful baking powder.

Rub sugar and butter together until very
light, beat up your egg whites very stiff,
add them to the butter and sugar little at
a time, mixing in lightly, add flavor and
mix, sift the flour and baking powder
together at least four times, mix in
lightly (do not whip), put in mould and
bake in very moderate oven an hour and a
half to two hours.

LADY CAKE No. 2

One pound flour.
Three-fourths pound sugar.
One-half pound butter.
One cup milk.
Whites of seven eggs.
Teaspoonful bitter almond flavor.
One tablespoonful baking powder.

Cream the sugar and butter, add the milk,
mixing in thoroughly, beat the egg whites
very stiff, add a little at a time, mixing
in lightly, add flavoring, sift the flour
and baking powder together at least four
times grease mould and line with paper

greased with unsalted butter, bake in slow
oven, one and one-half to two hours. When
cold ice and decorate to suit yourself.

ORANGE CAKE

Two pounds pulverized sugar. (ouch!)
Two and one-half pounds flour.
One and one-half pounds butter.
Sixteen eggs.
One tablespoonful vanilla.

Rub the sugar and butter together until
light and white, add the eggs two at a
time, whipping them in well with a good
strong egg whip, sift the baking powder
and flour together three or four times,
add, mixing in very lightly, add flavoring
and mix. Fill well greased mould, and bake
in slow oven, when cold ice with plain or
boiled icing.

SILVER CAKE

One pound butter.
One pound powdered sugar.
One pound, four ounces flour.
Whites of twenty eggs.
One teaspoonful baking powder.

Cream the sugar and butter, add the
flavoring and mix, beat the whites very
stiff, add a little at a time, mixing in
lightly, sift the flour and baking powder
together five times and mix in very light.

Grease mould and dust with flour, knock
out the surplus flour, line bottom with
paper and grease, bake in a slow oven,
about two hours.

GOLD CAKE

Two pounds flour.
One pound butter.
One pound, six ounces powdered sugar.
Yolks of twenty eggs.
One pint milk.
One and one-half ounces baking powder.
Two teaspoonful orange flavoring.

Sift the baking powder and flour together
at least three times. Cream the butter and
sugar, cream in the yolks adding two or
three at a time, then stir in the milk and
flavoring, then add the flour and mix
smooth, bake in square or triangular pans,
well greased and dusted with flour,
knocking out the loose flour. When cool,
ice with orange icing.

RAISIN POUND CAKE

One pound powdered sugar.
One pound good firm butter.
Ten eggs.
One pound, four ounces flour.
Teaspoonful lemon extract.
Two teaspoonful baking powder.
One and one-half pound sultana raisins.
Cream the butter and sugar, add the eggs
one or two at a time, whipping them in

with a good strong egg whip, rub the
raisins in flour, then shake off all
the loose flour, and add., mix in
thoroughly sift the flour and baking
powder together, then add and mix in fully
but lightly, bake in a cool oven about two
hours. When cold ice.

DIAMOND CAKE

Half pound good butter,
Twelve ounces powdered sugar.
Whites of ten eggs.
One cupful milk.
One pound flour.
One teaspoonful baking powder.
One teaspoonful vanilla.

Cream the butter and sugar, add the milk
and thoroughly mix, beat the egg whites
very stiff and mix in lightly, sift the
flour and baking powder together then mix
in fully but lightly, put in layer cake
tins that have been greased and dusted
with flour and the surplus flour knocked
out, bake in moderate oven. When cool, put
together with any filling you choose.

PLAIN WHITE POUND CAKE

One-half cup Butter.
One and one-half cups powdered sugar.
One cup milk.
Three cups flour.
Two teaspoonful baking powder.
Whites of six eggs.

Rub the sugar and butter together until
white and very light, put in the milk and
flavoring and thoroughly mix, sift the
flour and baking powder together two or
three times through a fine sieve, add and
mix in lightly, beat the egg whites very
stiff then mix in lightly but fully,
prepare mould and fill, bake in a moderate
oven, when cold ice,

CHEAP WHITE CAKE

One and one-half cups flour.
One cup sugar.
One-half cup butter.
Whites of four eggs.
One-half cup milk.
One teaspoonful baking powder.
One teaspoonful vanilla or almond.

Cream the sugar and butter, add the milk
and flavoring, mix in fully, beat the egg
whites very stiff, then mix in lightly,
sift the baking powder and flour together
and mix in fully but lightly. This can be
baked in a round or square mould, bake in
moderate oven, When cold ice with plain or
boiled icing.

HICKORY NUT CAKE

One and one-half pounds flour.
One pound sugar.
One-half pound hickory nut kernels.
Twelve ounces good butter.
Whites of twelve eggs.
Half pint sweet milk.
Teaspoonful lemon or vanilla.

Cream the butter and sugar, (if you have
it use pulverized sugar it works easier),
add the milk and mix, add chopped nuts and
flavoring and mix, sift the baking powder
and flour together at least four times,
mix in very lightly, beat the egg whites
stiff, mix in lightly but thoroughly, bake
in moderate oven.

WHITE NUT CAKE

One pound butter.
One pound powdered sugar.
One pound, four ounces flour.
Whites of ten eggs.
One cup of milk.
Four ounces finely chopped nuts.
One tablespoonful baking powder.
One teaspoonful lemon extract.

Cream the butter and sugar, add milk and
flavoring and mix, add nuts and mix, sift
the baking powder and flour together, mix
in lightly, beat the whites very stiff,
mix in lightly but thoroughly, prepare
your mould and fill, bake. When cool ice

with a good icing.

WALNUT CAKE

One pound butter.
One pound powdered sugar.
One pound, four ounces flour.
Four ounces finely chopped walnuts.
Ten eggs.
Two teaspoonful baking powder.
Almond flavoring.

Rub the butter and sugar together until
light and white, whip in the eggs adding
two at a time but be sure and whip them
light, add the chopped nuts and flavoring
and mix, sift the baking powder and flour
together, add and mix in lightly but
thoroughly, bake in shallow square pan or
regular pound cake mould, ice with plain
icing.

BIRTHDAY LAYER CAKE

Two cups powdered sugar.
Three-fourths cup butter.
Eight eggs.
Half cup milk.
Four cups flour.
Two teaspoonful baking powder.
Two teaspoonful allspice.
One teaspoonful cinnamon.
One teaspoonful ground cloves.
Four ounces raisins.

Four ounces citron cut fine.

Cream the butter and sugar, add the eggs
two at a time, whipping them in well, add
the milk and mix, mix in the flour fully
but lightly, divide this cake dough into
two equal parts, put one part into another
dish, add to one-half the allspice,
cinnamon, cloves, raisins and citron, mix
in lightly but thoroughly, make two layers
of the dark and two layers of the other,
and bake in a moderate oven. When cool put
together with a good icing, putting them
one layer of dark then a layer of light,
then a layer of dark, putting the last
layer of light on top, then ice the top
and side.

KING LAYER CAKE

One and a half pounds sugar.
Twelve ounces butter.
One pint milk.
Two pounds flour.
Whites of twelve eggs.
Three teaspoonful baking powder.
Two teaspoonful flavoring.

Rub the butter and sugar until it is very
light, beat the egg whites a little, then
add, a little at a time creaming them in,
add the milk a little at a time, mixing in
well, add the flavoring and mix, sift the
baking powder and sugar together, two to
five times and mix in fully but lightly,
bake in layers. These layers can be put

together with any icing or filling in this
book.

CHOCOLATE LAYER CAKE

Two cups sugar.
Half cup butter.
One cup sweet milk.
Five egg whites.
Two teaspoonful baking powder.
Two cupful flour.
One teaspoonful vanilla.

Cream the sugar and butter, add the cup
milk and the vanilla and mix in thoroughly
sift the baking powder and flour together,
add and mix in thoroughly, beat the egg
whites very stiff and mix in fully but
lightly, bake in layer cake tins that have
been properly prepared, when cool put
together with a chocolate filling, set in
the warmer a few minutes to harden.

PRINCESS LAYER CAKE

One pound powdered sugar.
One pound butter.
One pound, two ounces flour.
Whites of sixteen eggs.
One teaspoonful baking powder.
One and half teaspoonful flavor.

Cream the butter and sugar, beat the egg
whites to a very stiff froth, add a few at
a time, and mix in fully, then sift the
baking powder and flour together, at least

four times, mix in very lightly but
thoroughly, mix in vanilla fully but
lightly, bake in layer cake tins in a
moderate oven, when cold put together with
a good icing or filling.

SUNDAY LAYER CAKE

Three-fourths pound sugar.
Half pound butter.
Whites of ten eggs.
Half pint milk.
One pound, four ounces flour.
Two teaspoonful baking powder.
Teaspoonful vanilla.

Cream the butter and sugar, put the
vanilla in the milk and mix in a little at
a time, mixing fully, sift the baking
powder and the flour together four times,
mix in lightly. Whip the eggs up very
stiff, mix in lightly but fully, bake in
layer cake tins in a moderate oven, when
cold put together with a good filling or
icing.

COCONUT LAYER CAKE

Three-fourths pound powdered sugar.
Eight ounces butter.
Whites of ten eggs.
Half pint milk.
One pound flour.
Two teaspoonful vanilla.
Two teaspoonful baking soda.

Cream sugar and butter, beat egg whites
and add milk and flavoring, then add flour
with the two teaspoonful baking powder
sifted in it, bake in layer cake tins.
When cold put together as follows : Make a
good icing, put on a thin coat, sprinkle
with grated coconut, then ice the bottom
of the next layer and set it on the
coconut, repeat until all or fixed this
way, then ice top and side and sprinkle
with coconut.

MIXED LAYER CAKE

Three cupful powdered sugar.
One cupful of butter.
One cupful of milk.
Whites of five eggs.
Yolks of five eggs.
Four cups flour.
Three teaspoonful baking powder.
One or two teaspoonful flavoring.

Cream the sugar and butter, add the milk
and flavoring, mixing in thoroughly, sift
the baking powder and flour together and
mix in lightly. Now divide the dough into
two equal parts, beat the egg whites very
stiff and mix in to one part lightly, beat
the yolks well and mix into the other
part, bake in layer cake tins. When cold
put together with any icing or filling you
wish.

ORANGE LAYER CAKE

Two cups powdered sugar.
One cup good butter.
Five eggs.
One cup milk.
Two teaspoonful baking powder.
Two teaspoonful vanilla.
Three and one-half cupful flour.

Rub the butter and sugar to a cream, add
the eggs one at a time and cream in, add
the milk and flavoring, mixing in fully,
sift the baking powder and flour together
and mix in lightly but thoroughly, bake in
square pans that have been well greased
and dusted with flour, and the loose flour
knocked out. When cold put together with
the following filling:

Filling

Whites of two eggs.
One cup powdered sugar.
One Orange.

Grate the orange rind and all, take out
the seeds if there are any, put the sugar
in a pan add two tablespoonful water and
let boil until it threads from the spoon,
beat the eggs up very stiff, pour the
boiled sugar into them mixing all the
time, then put in the grated orange a
little at a time whipping it in, spread
two teaspoonful vanilla between and on top
the layers.

JELLY LAYER CAKE

Half cupful of butter.
One and one-half cupful sugar.
Two cupful flour.
Half cup milk.
Whites of two eggs.
Three teaspoonful baking powder.
Rub butter and sugar together until light,
add one egg one at a time and cream in,
add the milk and flavoring, mix in, sift
the baking powder and flour together, bake
in layer cake tins in a moderate oven
When cold put together with a good jelly.

CREAM LAYER CAKE

Whites of seven eggs.
One and one-half cupful sugar.
One cup sweet cream or half cupful butter
Half cupful of milk.
Two cupful flour.
Two teaspoonful baking powder.
One teaspoonful vanilla.

Rub the cream or butter and sugar until
light, add the other ingredients and mix
in fully but lightly, bake in layers and
when cold put together, with one cup
cream whipped to a froth sweetened and
flavored to taste. This cake should be
used at once as it will not keep long. The
cream filling will sour, but when used
immediately it makes a fine cake.

YELLOW LAYER

One and one-half pounds flour.
One pound sugar.
Half pound butter.
Three teaspoonful baking powder.
Eight eggs.
Three-fourths pint milk.
Two teaspoonful vanilla.
Rub the butter and sugar together until
white, and very light, beat the eggs and
add little at a time, mixing in
thoroughly, add flavoring and mix, sift
the baking powder and flour together and
add, mixing in fully but lightly, bake in
layer cake tins and put together with any
icing or filling you may choose.

PLAIN LAYER

One pound, two ounces flour.
Twelve ounces sugar.
Half pound butter.
Half pint milk.
Five eggs.
Two teaspoonful baking powder.
One teaspoonful vanilla extract.

Cream the sugar and butter, add the eggs
one at a time and cream in, add the milk
and flavoring little at a time, mixing in
fully, sift the baking powder and flour
together, two or three times, then add
mixing in lightly, bake in layers in a
moderate oven, when cold put together with
plain icing.

CHEAP PLAIN LAYER CAKE

One cupful sugar.
Four eggs.
Half cup butter.
One and one-half cupful flour.
Half cup milk.
One and one-half teaspoonful baking
powder.
One teaspoonful vanilla.

Cream the sugar and butter, add the eggs
one at a time, creaming in, add the milk
and flavoring mixing in well, sift the
flour and baking powder together and stir
in lightly but fully, bake in regular
layer cake tins, in moderate oven. When
cold put together with plain icing.

CHEAP LAYER CAKE

Half pound butter.
Twelve ounces sugar.
Whites of five eggs.
Three-fourths pint milk.
One pound flour.
Two teaspoonful baking powder.
One teaspoonful flavoring.

Rub the sugar and butter together until
very lights add the milk and flavoring a
little at a time, mixing in thoroughly,,
beat the whites stiff and add, mixing in
lightly but fully, sift the baking powder
and flour together, add mixing in lightly,

bake m layers and put together with any of
the icings or fillings.

FROSTINGS, ICINGS AND FILLINGS

The eggs should always be cold and the
platter on which they are beaten should be
cold.

HOW TO MAKE ICING

Break the eggs then put a handful sugar on
them, then commence beating, then keep
adding a little sugar at a time until all
is whipped in, this makes a nice smooth
icing.

HOW TO ICE CAKE

Take a long broad knife to spread it with,
and put on two coats, let the first be put
on thin and only to fill up the holes and
rough places, let this harden a little
then put on the last coat, wet the knife
occasionally to make it smooth. If the
icing is too soft and wants to run whip in
more sugar.

A little lemon juice, salt, soda, or
tartaric acid added to eggs before
commencing to beat, will make them beat
easier and some whiter.

If you wish to ornament save out part of
the icing and when the icing on the cake

is hard you can color it to suit yourself
and ice as you desire! Always set the cake
after icing in the warmer or in front of
the oven with the door open as soon as
iced this will dry the icing.

WATER ICING

Confectioner's sugar is the best sugar for
icing, it cost a little more but is
cheaper in the long run, as it takes up
more sugar.

Plain water icing is made by simply mixing
sifted powdered sugar with cold water.
Goods iced with this icing should be set
in the oven a few seconds to dry.

Boiled water icing is made by using
boiling water in place of cold. Goods iced
with this icing need not be returned to
the oven.

PLAIN ICING

Take the whites of two eggs and one cup
sugar, and whip thoroughly, if flavoring
is wanted add before commencing to beat.

PLAIN ICING No. 2

Beat the whites of two eggs very stiff,
add one cup of sugar and whip into the
eggs, add sugar little at a time.

BOILED ICING

Wet one cupful of sugar with a little
water, and let boil until it threads or
drops from a spoon or gets hard in water,
beat the whites of two eggs very stiff,
pour the sugar into the eggs, whipping all
the time.. If flavoring is wanted add to
taste.

FRESH FRUIT FILLING

Wash and pick over the fruit, then wash,
add enough powdered sugar to sweeten,
spread between the layers, ice the top.

PEACH CREAM FILLING

Take good ripe peaches, peel and cut in
thin slices lay on the cake and pour over
the peaches, sweet cream whipped to a
froth and sweetened with powdered sugar.

ORANGE FILLING

Grate one large or two small oranges, beat
the white of one egg with one cup powdered
sugar added, then add the grated orange
and whip in, spread between the layers.

FIG FILLING

To two cups finely chopped figs take one
cup sugar, add a little water and set on
the fire and let boil until the syrup
threads from the spoon, let set until
almost cool, then spread between the

layers.

FIG FILLING No. 2

Take two cups finely chopped figs and one
cup sugar and set on the fire and boil
until the syrup threads from the spoon,
then beat the whites of two eggs very
stiff, pour the figs into the eggs,
stirring all the time, spread between the
layers.

APPLE FILLING

Peel and slice some good cooking apples,
put them on the fire with sugar enough to
sweeten, when soft mash and run through a
fine sieve, add a small piece of butter
and the juice of one lemon or one teaspoonful lemon extract, when cold spread
between the layers.

BANANA FILLING

Take good ripe bananas that are free from
rotten and black places and mash up fine,
mix in a little sweet cream and enough
powdered sugar to sweeten, nut between the
layers.

NUT FILLING

One cupful sugar.
Whites of two eggs.
One cup chopped nuts.

Put the sugar in a pan add two teaspoonful
water, let boil until it threads from the
spoon, beat the whites stiff, pour the
boiled sugar into the eggs stirring all
the time, then stir the nuts in adding
them a little at a time and whipping them
in.

CHOCOLATE ICING OR FILLING

One cup milk.
One cup grated chocolate.
One and a half cups pulverized sugar.
Two eggs.
One teaspoonful vanilla.

Put the milk in a pan and set on the stove
and let come to a boil, then put the
grated chocolate in, when dissolved add
the sugar, beat the eggs a little and add
stirring fast, take from the stove and add
vanilla.

CHOCOLATE ICING OR FILLING No. 2

Half cup milk.
One cup powdered sugar.
Four ounces bakers chocolate.
One egg, or the whites of two.
One teaspoonful vanilla.

Grate the chocolate and put it in the milk
and set on the stove, when thoroughly
dissolved add the sugar and let boil until
it ropes off the spoon, take from the fire

and whip in the egg which has previously
been beaten, then add the vanilla, let
cool a little, it will then be ready for
use.

CHOCOLATE ICING No. 3

One and one-half cups sugar.
Half cup milk.
Half cake chocolate.
Half teaspoon vanilla.

Grate the chocolate and put in the milk
when thoroughly dissolved, add the sugar,
let boil until it ropes from the spoon,
take from the fire and add the vanilla.

LEMON ICING

Grate one lemon rind and all taking out
the seeds. Take one cup of sugar, add a
little water and set on fire and let boil
until it ropes or drops from the spoon,
beat the white of one egg stiff, pour in
the sugar, beating all the time, then beat
in the grated lemon.

MARSHMALLOW FILLING

Three-fourths cup sugar.
One-fourth cup milk.
One-fourth pound marshmallows.
Two tablespoonful hot water.
Half teaspoonful vanilla.

Put the hot water on the sugar and set on

the fire and let boil until it drops or
threads from the spoon, add the milk, then
the marshmallows, stirring them until
dissolved, let boil until it thickens a
little, take from the fire then, add the
vanilla, let cool a little then put
between the layers and on top and sides.

CARAMEL FILLING

Two cups brown sugar.
Tablespoonful butter.
One cup cream.
Two teaspoonful vanilla.

Dampen the sugar with a little water and
set on the fire and let boil a minute,
then stir in the butter, then the cream,
let boil until it gets hard, when dropped
in water, then remove from the fire and
put in the vanilla, stirring it in. Let
cool a little, it will then be ready to
put between the layers, on top and side,
set in the warmer or front part of the
stove a few minutes to dry.

SPONGE CAKE

Nine eggs
Half pound powdered sugar.
Twelve ounces flour.
Four ounces cornstarch.
Lemon or vanilla flavoring.

Beat the yolks of the eggs, then put in
bowl and cream in the sugar a little at a
time, then beat the egg whites very stiff
and add a few at a time, mixing in lightly
but thoroughly, mix in the flavoring, then
mix in the flour fully but lightly. Bake
slowly and well in paper lined tin, in a
moderate oven.

SPONGE CAKE No. 2

One pound powdered sugar.
Thirteen eggs.
One pound, two ounces flour.
Lemon flavoring.

Make the sugar lukewarm, add the eggs, one
or two at a time and wisk until they
assume a very light yellow color, then add
the flavoring beat in with a few
turns of the wisk, clean the side of the
pan and wisk in then clean the wisk, add
the flour, sifting it in slowly and mixing
it in fully but lightly, put in properly
prepared mould and bake in moderate oven.

Note. The colder the sponge is at time of
adding flour, the better the cake will be.

SHEET CAKE

One pound unwashed butter.
One pound, two ounces sugar.
Four eggs.
One pint milk.

Two pounds flour.
Two tablespoonful baking powder.
Lemon, almond or vanilla flavor.

Rub the butter and sugar to a cream, add
the eggs one at a time, and cream in, then
add the milk and mix, then the flavoring,
sift the baking powder and the flour
together and mix in, grease pan and dust
with flour, knock out the loose, then
fill, spread about one-half to one inch
thick on a level dust with powdered sugar
and bake.

NUT SHEET CAKE

Half pound butter.
Twelve ounces sugar.
One and one-fourth cups milk.
Three eggs.
One and one-fourth pounds flour.
Two teaspoonful baking powder.
One teaspoonful almond.
Chopped nuts to suit.

Cream the butter and sugar, cream in the
eggs one at a time, add the milk and
flavoring and mix in, sift the baking
powder and flour together and put in also,
put in the nuts and mix all in lightly but
fully, put in pan and spread about an inch
thick on the level, you can dust with
sugar if you like, bake in medium
hot oven.

FRUIT SHEET CAKE

Half pound butter.
Four eggs.
One and one-half pounds flour.
One and one-half cups milk.
One pound sugar.
Three teaspoonful baking powder.
Two teaspoonful almond.
Chopped raisins, currants or figs or all
to suit.

Cream sugar and butter, cream in eggs one
at a time, mix in milk and flavoring, put
in flour with baking powder sifted in it,
add fruit and mix in lightly but
thoroughly, bake in sheet pan in
moderately hot oven. If you wish you can
put whole raisins on top, or sprinkle with
sugar, or leave them off, just as you
like.

LADY FINGERS

One pound powdered sugar.
One pound flour.
Fifteen eggs.
Lemon flavor.

Beat the yolks and whites separately,
cream the sugar and egg yolks, adding the
yolks a little at a time, add flavoring,
then add the beaten whites, mixing in very
lightly, then add the flour mix in very
lightly but fully. Make a paper funnel

with half inch opening and fill with the
dough, run onto paper, in the shape of a
finger, dust with sugar and set on another
pan turned upside down, lady fingers
require heat from the top, when baked let
cool, then turn the paper over with the
cakes stuck to it and wet with water turn
back and lift the fingers off, stick two
together.

LADY FINGERS No. 2

One pound powdered sugar.
Whites of twelve eggs.
Yolks of six eggs. :
Two teaspoonful lemon extract.
One teaspoonful baking powder.

Beat the yolks, then cream the sugar and
yolks together, add the yolks to the
sugar, little by little until all in, add
the flavoring, and mix, sift the baking
powder with one cup of flour, and mix in
just a little, beat the egg whites very
stiff, mix in very lightly but fully, then
add enough more flour to make a soft dough
(make dough just as soft as you can handle
it) roll out to about half inch thick and
cut with lady finger cutter, set in pan
lined with brown paper, dampen tops with
water and sprinkle with powdered sugar,
bake in moderate oven, when cold turn
paper over and wet bottom side of cakes,
turn back, pull cakes off and stick two
together.

JELLY ROLL

Twelve eggs.
One pound sugar.
One pound, two ounces flour.
One ounce baking powder.
Vanilla flavor.
Whip the sugar and eggs together until
very light, then stir in flour, baking
powder and flavoring, bake in thin sheet
and spread with jelly and roll up.

JELLY ROLL No. 2

Seven eggs.
Twelve ounces sugar.
Twelve ounces flour.
One teaspoonful baking powder.

Flavor to suit, proceed same as for
ordinary jelly roll.

STRAWBERRY SHORT CAKE.

One pound butter.
One pound, four ounces flour.
Six eggs.
Half pint milk.
Half pound butter
Two to three teaspoonful baking powder,
Strawberry flavor.

Rub the sugar and butter together, add the
eggs one at a time and rub in, stir in the
milk and flavoring, then sift the baking

powder and flour together and mix in, bake
in layer cake tins, then take strawberries
and cover a layer sprinkle sugar over them
and put on another layer and repeat the
operation and the cake is ready to serve.

STRAWBERRY SHORT CAKE No. 2

One pound flour.
Four ounces butter or lard.
One tablespoonful sugar.
Pinch salt.
Three teaspoonful baking powder.

Water or milk enough to make a medium
stiff dough, mix same as the tea biscuit,
then proceed same as other short cake,
only you split the layer and put
berries between and on top.

CREAM PUFFS

Take one pint of water and half cupful
milk, mix together, add eight ounces lard
and set on the fire and let come to a
boil, let boil two minutes. But be sure
it boils, then stir into it one pound cake
flour, stir in until all is loosened from
the pan and dry, then remove from the
fire, stir in twelve eggs whipping them in
two at a time, add a little baking powder.
Bake on pans washed with egg, bake rapid
in a medium hot oven. Cut open and fill
with custard or whipped cream,

VANILLA WAFERS

Ten ounces sugar.
One pound butter.
One pint sweet milk.
Four eggs.
One pound flour.
Two teaspoonful baking powder.
Two teaspoonful vanilla.

Rub butter and sugar to a cream, then rub
in eggs - one at a time, add milk and
flavoring and mix in, then sift the baking
powder and flour together and mix...
proceed as for other wafers.

LEMON SNAPS

One pound powdered sugar.
Three eggs.
One pound flour.
Three ounces butter.
Teaspoonful baking powder.
Lemon.

Rub the butter and sugar together, add
eggs and cream in, add lemon and mix, then
sift the baking powder in the flour and
mix in well, roll out in round rope like
and cut off in little pieces the size of
walnuts, place on greased pans about three
inches apart and flatten with the hands,
bake in a cool oven.

DROP CAKES

Ten ounces sugar.
Six ounces butter and lard mixed.
Four eggs.
Half pint milk.
One pound flour.
Two teaspoonful baking powder.
One teaspoonful vanilla.

Cream the sugar and butter, add the eggs
one at a time and cream in, mix in milk
and flavoring, then sift the baking powder
in the flour and mix in fully but lightly.
This dough should be dropped from a spoon,
or canvas bag made for this purpose, the
heat while baking makes them run, bake in
a moderate oven.

TEA CAKES

Four eggs.
One cup butter or lard.
Two and one-half cupful sugar.
One cupful milk.
Two and one-half teaspoonful baking
powder.
One teaspoonful almond extract.

Rub to a cream the butter, eggs and sugar,
then add the milk, mix in fully, add the

flavoring, sift the baking powder in a
little flour and add, then add enough more
flour to make a medium stiff dough, roll
out, cut with round cutter and set apart
in pans so they will not stick together.
Brush the loose flour off the top and bake
in moderate oven.

COOKIES

One cup butter.
Three-fourths cup lard.
Two cupful sugar.
One cupful sour milk.
One level teaspoonful soda.
Two eggs.
Two teaspoonful flavoring.

Rub the sugar, butter and lard to a cream,
dissolve the soda in the sour milk and mix
in thoroughly, beat the eggs and add, add
flavoring and mix in, then add enough
flour to make a medium stiff dough, roll
out with rolling pin and cut with round
cutter, brush the surplus flour off and
bake.

*Note. Always set cookies apart, giving
them room to run while baking.*

SUGAR COOKIES

One pound sugar.
Half pound lard.
Two eggs.

One-half pint milk.
Three tablespoonful water.
Two teaspoonful baking powder.
For flavoring you can use any of the
following;
Lemon, vanilla, almond, strawberry,
banana,
mace, nutmeg or cinnamon.
Two pounds, four ounces sugar.

Rub together the sugar, lard and eggs, add
the milk, water and flavoring, and mix,
sift the baking powder in the flour and
mix in, roll out when you have it almost
thin enough, brush the flour off and
sprinkle with sugar, then roll to thinness
desired, cut out and bake.

CHOCOLATE COOKIES

Half cup milk.
Half cupful butter.
Half cupful lard.
One cupful of sugar.
Four eggs.
One teaspoonful baking powder.
One teaspoonful vanilla.
One-half cup grated chocolate.

Cream the lard, butter and sugar, then add
the eggs and cream in, add the milk and
mix in thoroughly, add the vanilla and
grated chocolate and mix in fully, then
add enough flour to make a medium stiff
dough, roll out thin and cut with round

cutter, bake in moderate oven. If you will
wash the tops with milk before baking,
they will be nicer.

RAISIN COOKIES

Four cups flour.
One and one-half cups butter.
One cup sugar.
Six eggs.
Two teaspoonful baking powder.
One teaspoonful vanilla.
One cup seedless or sultana raisins.

Rub together the sugar and butter until
light, add the eggs two at a time,
creaming them in, add flavoring and mix,
sift the baking powder and flour together,
rub the raisins in the flour, then add and
mix in thoroughly but lightly, finish same
as other cookies. You can leave the
raisins out, and wash top with milk and
stick the raisins on top.

CUP CAKES

Two cups sugar.
One cup butter.
Six eggs.
Eight cups flour.
One and one-half cups milk.
One and one-half tablespoonful baking
powder.

Flavor with lemon or almond.

Cream the butter, and sugar, then cream in
the eggs, then add the milk and flavoring,
mix well, then add the flour and finish
mixing, if too stiff add milk to make a
medium slack mass, bake in cup cake tins,
in a good solid heat, sprinkle the top
with currants before baking.

ROYAL GINGER CAKE

Three-fourths pound butter.
Three-fourths pound sugar.
Four eggs.
One pound flour.
Teaspoonful ground ginger.
Teaspoonful ground cinnamon.
Teaspoonful lemon flavoring.
One cup milk.
One teaspoonful baking powder.

Cream the butter, sugar, eggs, ginger,
cinnamon and flour together, add the milk
and mix it in, then add the flour with the
baking powder sifted in it and mix fully
but lightly, if baked as loaf cake, dust
top with sugar and sprinkle with water, or
if baked in layers put together with
icing.

GINGER BREAD

One-half pound butter.

Eight ounces brown sugar.
Four eggs.
One ounce ground ginger.
One pint molasses.
One pint milk.
Two to three teaspoonful soda.
Two and one-half pounds flour.

Cream the butter, sugar, eggs and ginger,
add the molasses and mix in thoroughly,
dissolve the soda in the milk and add,
mixing fully, add the flour, mixing
in lightly but thoroughly, put in well
greased pan and bake in cool oven,

GINGER SNAPS

Eight ounces lard.
Eight ounces sugar.
One cup molasses.
One-half cup water.
Two pounds, four ounces flour.
One ounce soda.
One ounce ginger.

Cream the molasses, sugar and lard, add
the water with the soda dissolved in it,
and mix well, mix in the ginger then mix
in the flour, work well, roll out thin and
cut with small cutter, wash pans with
water, and wash snaps on top with water
before baking.

CORN MIXTURE

Pop your corn and sieve it with a sifter
that has holes large enough to let the un-
popped corn fall through. Then place in
your kettle one pound of sugar, put on
just enough water to start it to boiling,
let boil a little while then add one
cupful molasses, let boil until it drops
from a spoon or gets hard when dropped in
water, then take from the fire and add
tablespoonful butter, then stir in your
popped corn and a little salt, stir in all
the popcorn you can, then set your kettle
on fire to warm slightly, turn out on slab
and shape into squares or balls just as
you like.

SALTED ALMONDS

Soak the almonds in warm water, then take
the skin off, set in a warm place and let
thoroughly dry. Put about half cup butter
in a sauce pan and set on fire, when hot
put in about one pound of almonds and
stir them until a light brown color, then
take them out and allow the butter to
drain off, then mix them in dry salt, then
sift off the excess salt and set away to
cool and dry.

PEANUT CANDY

Take two pounds of brown sugar and put in
pan add just a little water, set on fire
and let come to a boil, then add one pound
peanuts, let cook until when you drop some

of it in cold water you can chew it
without sticking to your mouth, then stir
in a little soda. But be sure there are no
lumps in the soda. Pour into greased
plates and allow to cool.

PEANUT CANDY

Take two cups brown sugar and put in pan,
add a little water and set on the stove
where it is not very hot, until the sugar
is dissolved, then push to a hot place and
let come to a boil, add a little piece of
butter and one cupful peanuts, let boil
until it ropes from the spoon, then take
from the fire and whip it as fast as you
can and until it is almost cold, then put
in buttered plates and let cool.

NUT CANDY

Put two cups of brown sugar in a sauce
pan, add a little water and set on the
fire and let come to a boil, add a small
piece of butter and let cook until it gets
hard when you drop a little in cold water,
then add one teaspoonful vanilla and the
nuts remove from the fire and whip until
it begins to get cold, then put into
greased plates and set aside to cool.

VANILLA SUGAR CANDY

Put two cups granulated sugar and half cup
vinegar in sauce pan and let cook. You
must be careful and cook it just right, to

test it drop a little in a half cup cold
water from time to time when it gets hard
and will just snap into without stringing,
it is done. Take from the fire and add two
teaspoonful vanilla, pour into buttered
plates and let cool just a little, then
take it out of the plates and pull it
until white and cold.

BAKING POWDER

The following is a good recipe. If you
wish to make your own, however, it is just
about as cheap to buy a good brand.

One pound cream of tartar.
One and one-half pound carbonate of soda.
Eight ounces tartaric acid.
Four ounces corn starch.

Put each one in a warm place and let dry
thoroughly, then sift through a fine sieve
several times, this mixes them thoroughly,
put in cans and keep in a dry place.

ENJOY!!!!

Made in the USA
Monee, IL
08 July 2026

56679420R00069